E. M. Wherry

Islam or the Religion of the Turk

E. M. Wherry

Islam or the Religion of the Turk

ISBN/EAN: 9783744785006

Printed in Europe, USA, Canada, Australia, Japan

Cover: Foto ©Lupo / pixelio.de

More available books at **www.hansebooks.com**

ISLAM;

OR, THE

RELIGION OF THE TURK.

BY

REV. E. M. WHERRY, D. D.

———

AMERICAN TRACT SOCIETY,
10 EAST 23d ST., NEW YORK.

ISLAM;

OR, THE

RELIGION OF THE TURK.

THE recent atrocities in Armenia have served to bring to our notice the religion of Islam. The spectacle of a mighty potentate deliberately planning the destruction of myriads of his subjects has filled the civilized world with horror and indignation. The calm deliberation with which these plans have been executed has been no less awful to contemplate. Many have been ready to doubt the harrowing details of cities pillaged, men murdered, women outraged, and helpless girls carried captive to be enslaved in a Moslem harem. And when the Sultan at Constantinople calmly denies that these outrages have been com-

3

mitted, and yet continues them at frequent intervals, coolly daring the nations of Europe to intervene, our indignation is thoroughly aroused. We ask ourselves how men who profess themselves to be the servants of the merciful God can be the perpetrators of such fiendish cruelty: we wonder how men can be at once so religious and yet so devilish.

The enigma of the Turkish character finds its solution in his religion. The sword is consecrated to the cause of Islam. It may be unsheathed to repel an enemy or to make a convert. All Christians are regarded as idolaters, who may be destroyed at any time without sin whenever the interests of Islam require their removal. " Kill the idolaters," said the prophet, " wheresoever ye shall find them, and take them prisoners, and besiege them, and lay wait for them in every convenient place. But if they shall repent, and observe the appointed times of prayers, and pay the legal

4

alms, dismiss them freely." Quran, chap. IX., 5. The fact, then, that any Christians have been permitted to live in a country under Moslem rule is evidence to the Moslem that he has exercised a marvellous magnanimity. If then the Christian subject busy himself with political questions, and endeavor in any way to secure for himself a liberty denied by his Moslem ruler, he lays himself open to the charge of being a rebel, and so may be treated as an enemy of God and of the faithful. Accordingly the Sultan, with the advice and authority of the Moslem hierarchy, may order the slaughter of the men, giving them, however, the alternative of accepting the religion of Islam. In case the Christian select death rather than apostasy, his wife and children may be enslaved and his property seized as the spoil of war.

We have, therefore, in the Armenian massacres an object-lesson in the Moslem's religion. Two hundred millions of the earth's inhabitants are adherents to this faith, which is to-day the only rival of Christianity for supremacy in the world. The Sultan of Turkey for more than four hundred years has been recognized as the Defender of the Faith, the Caliph or vicegerent of God on earth. Forty millions of his own subjects bow the knee to his authority both as temporal and spiritual ruler. Fifty millions in India, besides millions more in Central Asia and North Africa, acknowledge his authority in matters of religion. These figures suggest some of the elements of complication which beset every effort to solve the Eastern Question. The religion of Islam is still a mighty force, which must be taken into account in any study of the political situation in the East. It is true that "the sick man" at Constantinople sometimes seems ready to die, but history tells of more than one marvellous recovery. The jealousy of the Christian powers may yet afford him another opportunity to rise and secure a new lease of life.

It goes without saying that the church cannot afford to be indifferent to the religion of the millions of Moslems in the midst of whom our devoted missionaries are living and laboring, in hope that by and by the gospel may find entrance to their hearts. Is it not the part of wisdom as well as the instinct of piety to endeavor to understand these remarkable people and to acquaint ourselves with the principles of their religion? By so doing we may perhaps better understand their place in the history of God's providential government of the world. Possibly we may learn something more of the way by which these worshippers of Allah, " the merciful and the beneficent," may become the followers of " the Christ, the Son of the living God !" It is with the hope of aiding in this cause that the writer presents the following brief popular statement of the faith and practice of the religion of Islam.

In the mind of the ordinary Christian the religion of Islam is a religion of yesterday. Unlike Brahminism or Buddhism, it inspires nothing of that veneration which is born of the glamor of antiquity. To him it is the religion of Mohammed the impostor. He sees little or no connection between it and his own faith or the faith of his fathers. To him the chief characteristics of the Moslem's creed are his faith in Allah and in Mohammed, the prophet of God, and his belief in his right to practise polygamy, adding to this his fanatical zeal in warfare against " infidels."

Not so with the Moslem himself. To him Islam is the only true religion : the religion vouchsafed to Adam, to Seth and Enoch, to Noah and Abraham, to Moses and the patriarchs, to David and all the prophets, to Jesus and his apostles, and finally to Mohammed, the last of the prophets. To him this religion comprehends all dispensations. It is the religion of the genii and of angels. It shall only find its consummation in eternity, amid the joys of paradise.

Looking at it from another standpoint, Islam may be called the religion of Submission to God. A Mussulman is one who has submitted himself to God, or, as Mohammedan doctors define it, " one who has placed his neck under the yoke of God." This religion, then, like that of the Jew and the Christian, is an exclusive religion. It admits none other as true. It knows no generous rivalry. There is, therefore, no foundation in fact for the theory of certain Christian writers that Islam and Christianity are destined, under a more liberal interpretation of their respective symbols of faith, to go hand in hand and shoulder to shoulder in a crusade against idolatry. That theory is an idle dream. There can be no such reconcilement. One must triumph over the fall of the other. So far, then, as the missionary problem is concerned, it means war to the end; war, however, with spiritual weapons against carnal: the sword of the Spirit against the sword of Islam.

In order to understand the faith of Islam let us examine its fundamental principles.

Moslem authors tell us of four *Irkan* or Pillars of the faith: the *Quran*, the *Ahadis* or traditions, the *Ijma*, or unanimous consent of the learned, and *Qiyas*, or analogical reasoning based upon the Quran, Ahadis, and Ijma. Let us examine these separately.

I. The Quran.

This is called by the Moslem *al Quran al Majid*, "the glorious Quran;" *al Quran ash-sharif*, "the noble Quran;" *al Furqan*, or "the Distinguisher;" and the *Kalam-Ullah*, or "the World of God." The original, they say, is inscribed upon the *Luh-i-Mahfuz*, or "Preserved Table," which is kept under the throne of God.* From this it was copied and sent down by the angel Gabriel. It follows that Mohammed, in the apprehension of his followers, was merely the mouthpiece of God in all he said.

The story of Mohammed's call to "recite" the Quran is one which is listened to with awe by millions of his followers. For some weeks Mohammed had been living as a recluse in a cave near the City of Makkah. One day he came to his wife Khadijah in great trepidation and fear, saying, "Wrap me up, wrap me up!" She wrapped him up until his fear was dispelled, when he told her the cause of his fear and trembling. He said that the angel Gabriel had come to him and said, "Read." He replied, "I am not a reader." "Then," said Mohammed, "the angel took hold of me and squeezed me as much as

---

* This notion of the Moslems may have arisen from the practice of the Jews of keeping the Sacred Book by the side of the ark in the Holy of Holies. Deut. 31:26; cf. 2 Kings 22:8.

I could bear, and he let me go and said, 'Read.' And I said, 'I am not a reader.' Then he took hold of me a third time and squeezed me as much as I could bear, and said,

"'Read! in the name of thy Lord who created man.

"'Read! for thy Lord is most beneficent;

"'He hath taught men the use of the pen;

"'He hath taught man that which he knoweth not.'"

Hearing this story the faithful Khadijah addressed herself to the work of comforting her husband. To his fears lest he should die, or lest he were the subject of some demoniacal possession, she said, "No, it will not be so. I swear by God he will never make you melancholy or sad. For verily you are kind to your relatives, you speak the truth, you are faithful in trust, you bear the afflictions of the people, you spend in good works what you gain in trade, you are hospitable, and you assist your fellow-men." She then took him to her cousin Waraqah, who was reputed a holy man and acquainted with the Jewish Scriptures. Said Waraqah, " Oh, son of my brother, what do you see ?" Then the prophet told him what he saw, and Waraqah said, " That is the Namus which God sent to Moses;" thereby expressing the idea that he was the subject of divine inspiration.

Such was the beginning of Mohammed's prophetic career. From this time forth during the space of a score of years the prophetic declarations of this remarkable man were recorded and carefully treasured up as the very words of God. They were given piecemeal, ever colored by the experiences of the prophet and the environments of the faithful. They were usually announced when some exigency of the new faith or of the personal interest of the prophet required. At Makkah the spirit of this prophecy anathematized the idols in the national pantheon, vindicating the unity of the Godhead by reference to the testimony of nature and the consciences of men. The tribe of the Quraish, which was the principal tribe of Makkah and the custodian of the sacred Kaabah, or temple, naturally resented this preaching. They ridiculed the prophet as a madman. They persecuted his followers, Mohammed himself being protected by powerful relations. The Quran carefully notes these facts, rebukes and threatens the persecutors. It tells them of the experiences of former prophets—how the unbelievers mocked and persecuted, how a merciful God warned them, how he even wrought miracles before them, and yet how the hardened wretches rushed blindly on to destruction. Some were swallowed up by an earthquake, others were drowned in the flood. Once a hot wind suddenly breathed upon a slumbering city, leaving its inhabitants corpses.

Again, a plague dealt out merited
destruction upon the enemies of
the Lord and his prophets. Again,
when the Jews opposed they were
warned by the fate of unbelievers
among them in the olden time.

At Madina the circumstances of
the prophet were entirely changed
and the character of the revelations of the Quran also changed.
At first the prophecy was concilia-
tory. The Jews were flattered.
The Moslems were commanded to
pray toward Jerusalem. Much was
said in praise of the Old Testament
saints. Thus did Mohammed hope
to win the children of Israel. But
the Jews were not inclined to rec-
ognize this new apostle. They
ridiculed his prophetic pretensions
and rejected him as an impostor.
The spirit of Quranic prophecy
now anathematized the Jews, and
declared them to be accursed of
God because they had persecuted
and slain his prophet. The temple at Jerusalem was rejected as
the Qibla, and Makkah was chosen

as the point towards which the faithful should pray. Christians were now spoken of kindly. They were said to be charitable. Jesus was declared to be a prophet of God. His purity of character and wonderful miracles were extolled.

By this time the new faith had gained many adherents — Arabs, Jews and Christians. A new adversary now arose ; it was Abdullah Ibn Ubbai, the chief of one of the most powerful factions in Madina, who was jealous of the influence of the prophet with his ever-increasing band of Moslems. Henceforth Abdullah and his party received the special attention of the inspiring genius of Mohammed. The necessities of inspiration increased, and now the voice of Gabriel was ever heard ringing in the ear of the prophet. Sometimes (as he said) it was like the sound of a bell, sometimes like the roar of a tornado ; at other times the angel in the form of one of Mohammed's attendants (Dahiyah) addressed him in audible voice. Now a command was given to make war upon the Makkah caravans. Then an order came relating to the Moslems—perhaps to regulate their social intercourse, their treatment of their wives, their neighbors, or their prophet. At another time prayer and fasting were instituted. Again, some ancient Arab custom was abolished. For example, the prophet fell in love with the beautiful Zainab, the wife of Zaid, his adopted son. Zaid, moved by devotion to his benefactor, was willing to divorce her; yea, in the face of Mohammed's protest, he did divorce her, that she might become the wife of the prophet. But, however willing the prophet and his devoted children, the custom of the Arab nation was against them. It was a scandalous thing for a man to marry the divorced wife of an adopted son. Here, then, the spirit of Mohammed's prophecy came to the rescue. A revelation was vouchsafed to the prophet commanding him to marry Zainab. This was done, said the prophecy, "in order that henceforth the faithful may not be bound by the old custom forbidding men to marry the divorced wives of their adopted sons."*

On another occasion a scandal arose in respect to waging war during the Sacred Months. From time immemorial Arab custom had made warfare unlawful during these months. The sword was sheathed. The bow and the shield were hung up within the tent doors. Enemies met without fear of danger to either life or property. Even the murderer of a father or a brother was safe in the companionship of the avenger of blood. It so happened that a small band of Moslem marauders found a Makkan caravan quietly encamped by a well at the beginning of the sacred season. Being off their guard they fell an easy prey to the Mos-

* See Quran, chap xxxiii., 37.

lems, who carried off the whole of their goods as the spoil of war. The Arab unbelievers and hypocrites of Madina made a great outcry at this outrage. The Moslems themselves were scandalized. Mohammed was blamed, inasmuch as the expedition has been undertaken by his order. The influence of the prophet was jeopardized. Seizing the marauders he placed them in ward. The spoil was placed in bond until such time as the will of God might be made known. The delay was not long. Gabriel appeared to the prophet, declaring that infidelity was worse than warfare in the Sacred Months and that henceforth the unbelievers would not be spared even during this season. Accordingly the prisoners were released and rewarded, while the booty was distributed among the faithful.

Again, an expedition was to be undertaken against the Jews: the order was given through the medium of the Quran. Some rude

Arabs showed undue familiarity in their approach to Mohammed: a revelation was vouchsafed regulating the manner of approach to the prophet of God. The character of Ayesha, the favorite wife of Mohammed, was aspersed and the prophet scandalized: the word of the Quran exonerated the favorite wife and prescribed punishment for the calumniators. Such is the character of the revelations of this book. So intimate is the relation between the matter of the revelations of the Quran and the life and experience of Mohammed that a knowledge of the latter is necessary to any intelligent understanding of the former.

At the death of Mohammed the various portions of the Quran were found in a box which had been committed to the care of one of his wives. They were written upon palm leaves and white stones. Many of the Moslems too possessed copies of portions and some of them had committed the whole to mem-

ory. The fatalities of war, however, led to the rapid thinning out
of the ranks of the *hafizes*, as those
were called who had committed the
Quran to memory. Under these
circumstances Zaid-Ibn-Sabit was
appointed by the Caliph (Khalifah)
Abu Baqr to compile the Quran.
This work he did, collecting all the
portions he could find from the
palm leaf and stone copies and
from those who repeated what they
knew as he recorded it for preser-
vation. The result was the volume
which we now possess. True, this
copy underwent some revision in
the Caliphate of Othman, but
only so as to make the idiom
everywhere to correspond to that
of the Quraishite tribe of Makkah.

This book contains 114 *suras* or
chapters. Those are not, however,
recorded in their chronological order, but, somewhat after the manner of the prophetical books of the
Jewish Scriptures, the longer chapters were placed first and the short-

er last—the whole being introduced
by a prayer.

This prayer reads as follows :

" In the name of God most merciful. Praise be to God, the Lord
of all creatures, the most merciful,
the king of the day of judgment.
Thee do we worship, and of thee
do we beg assistance. Direct us in
the right way, in the way of those
to whom thou hast been gracious ;
not of those against whom thou art
incensed, nor of those who go
astray."

This passage is perhaps the most
striking, if not the most beautiful
passage in the Quran. It reveals
to us at least two important reasons why the Quran holds such an
influence over the minds of two
hundred millions of the human
race. The first reason is the beautiful rhythm, and often sweet cadences of the original language.
They sound like the notes of some
enchanting song, holding multitudes with rapt attention who understand scarcely a word they hear.

The second reason is the vast amount of truth contained in the book; especially the truth of the divine unity and of man's dependence on God for salvation.

There are three points in the faith of Moslems concerning the Quran which we should not fail to notice here.

The first is the *doctrine of the eternity of the Quran.* According to this doctrine, the Quran is uncreated. The paper, ink, etc., of which the volume is formed are acknowledged to be creatures, even the forms of the letters are made, but the *Word of God* contained in this volume and represented by these forms is by all orthodox Moslems regarded as eternally existent in the mind of God; eternal as to its original essence. It is not God, yet it is inseparable from God.

The second point of faith in regard to the Quran relates to the *authority of the Quran.* In the light of the doctrine just mentioned we will be prepared to understand the value placed upon every jot and tittle of this book. It may only be read by "the pure." The text must be preserved unchanged. The words and letters are all counted. Holy men commit it to memory. Every question of doctrine is tested by its teaching. A single text is sufficient to establish any article of faith.

The third doctrine concerning the Quran which we would notice here is called the *doctrine of Abrogation*. It sprang up during the lifetime of Mohammed. It grew out of the necessities of his prophetic pretensions. Circumstances changed from time to time and changes in the revelation became necessary. Wherefore each new revelation was declared to abrogate the old whenever it was contrary to it.

This doctrine of abrogation has been worked up into a science. By modern Moslems it is made to apply to the former Scriptures, so that they do not hesitate to say that the Jewish Scriptures were abrogated by the Christian Scriptures, and these in turn by the Quran.

With this volume in hand the proud Moslem wants no other. It contains for him not only the truth, but, including the traditions, it contains all truth, so far as religion is concerned.

The story is told of the Caliph Omar that, when asked what should be done with the celebrated Alexandrian Library, he replied: " If the books therein agree with the Quran they are not needed : if they are contrary to it they should be destroyed." This story illustrates the ordinary estimate of the Moslem for the Christian Scriptures. Wherein they differ from the Quran it is said to be due to corruption by interpolation or forgery, so that they are only to be recognized in so far as they agree with the Quran. The consequence is that while the Quran attests the genuineness and credibility of the Bible yet Moslems hold that present copies are not trustworthy, and hence, because they contradict the Quran, they are to be rejected.

II. The next pillar of Islam is closely related to the Quran and yet differs materially from it. This pillar is called *Ahadis*, or Traditions. These are also called the *Sunnat*. They consist of the sayings, doings, and permissions of Mohammed in regard to various matters. They were collected two or three centuries after the death of the prophet. They represent (1) things said by Mohammed ; (2) things done by Mohammed in the presence of his disciples, and (3) things done by disciples in the prophet's presence against which he did not show any disapprobation ; (4) things done in the presence of Mohammed which he condemned. The mass of matter has been compiled in six ponderous tomes known as the "*as-Sihah-us-Sittah* (the Six Correct Books).

The principles which were applied, to decide between the genuine and spurious traditions, were peculiar. Collectors carefully examined the chain, not of evidence for and against the traditions, but of the persons relating them. If each link in the chain of witnesses were a pious Moslem of sound mind, discreet, sober and clearheaded, his testimony was accepted. If all the witnesses were thus reliable the tradition was accepted. Whenever there was a doubt as to one or more of the witnesses the tradition, though accepted, was marked as " weak " or " doubtful." It will be evident to all that under such circumstances the science of interpreting the traditions is no small part of a Moslem's education for the priesthood.

The following extract, from a famous collection of Moslem traditions entitled " The Tirmizi," will give the reader an idea of the form and character of these traditions:

" Abu Kuraib said to us that

Ibrahim ibn Yusuf ibn Abi Ishaq
said to us, from his father, from
Abu Ishaq, from Tulata ibn Musa-
rif that he said, I have heard, from
'Abdu'r-Rahman ibn Ausajah, that
he said I have heard that the
prophet said, *Whosoever shall give
in charity a milch cow, or silver, or a
leathern bottle of water, it shall be
equal to the freeing of a slave."*
It will be noted that a complete
chain of witnesses is here present-
ed between the prophet and the
final narrator of the tradition.

As the Quran is the chief source
of authority in doctrine, so the
traditions are the principal source
of knowledge in respect to all questions of practice. Not only is this
true of the ceremonies and customs relating to the daily and
other stated prayers, to the fast
of the Ramzan or the observ-
ances of the Muharram, to almsgiving and pilgrimage, but to the
customs relating to marriage and
death, to the usages of social and
family intercourse and even to all

matters of dress and adornments, down to the cut of the beard, the dye for the hair, and the particular wood to be used in making a toothbrush! All questions as to purification and washing are settled by reference to the traditions. Suppose, for instance, a dog should be drowned in a well, the question would immediately arise as to how that well could be rendered ceremonially clean. Learned men would be consulted, who would in turn consult the books and proceed to enlighten the minds of their co-religionists how many gallons of water must be drawn from the well before it can be regarded as having been purified. Never did Jewish scribes display more learning in adducing the sayings of the rabbis and doctors to prove some question as to washing of hands and cleaning of pots than do the Mullahs and learned men of Islam when discussing similar questions to-day.

III. The third pillar of Moslem

faith is called *Ijma.* This term expresses to the Moslem about the idea conveyed to a Christian by the expression "consensus of the fathers." It is a collection of the opinions of the Mujtahiddin or learned among the companions of the prophet, the Ansars, or helpers, who were converted at Madina during Mohammed's ministry there, and the disciples and companions of both of these classes. Naturally it was thought that such men were in a position best to understand what was meant by the words of the Quran, and especially by the sayings of their prophet preserved in the traditions. These opinions of the learned, however, must on no account contradict the teaching of the Quran or the traditions, but when they agree with these they are regarded as authority in all questions of interpretation and law.

IV. The fourth pillar of Moslem faith is called *Qiyas.* By this term is meant the analogical reasoning of the learned as to the teaching of the Quran, traditions and the Ijma. Here we find for the first time a place for the exercise of the reason. And yet even here how little is that exercise. The learned Imaums and Mujtahiddin of the first three centuries of Islam made certain deliverances, based upon the teachings of the Quran and traditions, which have been recorded for the guidance of the faithful. Since that time the "learned" among the orthodox have no successors, so that for centuries Moslem scholars have not striven to learn what the Quran and the Ahadis really teach, but to discover what the "learned" say they teach. Reason has virtually been ruled out of court. Dogmatism in the worst sense of that term has obtained almost absolute supremacy over Moslem minds. A hierarchy of the Uluma or learned doctors holds sway with a power rarely ever held by Pope or college of cardinals in the Romish Church.

Clothed with all the authority of the temporal power this hierarchy is able to mete out the severest penalties upon any and all who should dare to call in question their conclusions in regard to any matter of doctrine or practice. When the bastinado and the filthy dungeon fail to correct the contumacious, the bowstring and the axe avail. This survey of the fundamental doctrines of Islam will make clear to the reader its extreme rigidity. Everything is, as it were, fossilized. There is no room for development. The Moslem priest ever points to the past. Freedom of thought is denied him. No commentator may tell what he thinks the sacred writings teach, but, like the Pharisees of old, he declares in solemn tones what some old doctor taught one thousand years ago.

There are some ardent admirers of Turkish and Indian Moslems who entertain the hope that contact with the West and acquaint-

ance with its civilization will lead
to a reformation of their religion.
They seem to be looking for a
kind of Moslem millennium, when
the dignity of womanhood will be
acknowledged, when polygamy will
be abolished, when the slaves will
be set free and the accursed traffic
in human flesh be ended, when
reason and conscience shall be un-
trammeled and when Moslem and
Christian shall kneel in loving em-
brace at the Mercy Seat. Such
dreamers understand little of the
religion of the Moslem. The truth
is, the evils so notorious in Moslem
countries, and which have just
been mentioned, are sanctioned by
Islam. Slavery and polygamy,
with their contempt for the wail
of the slave and the degradation
of woman, will continue so long
as the Quran has authority over
the minds of men. No less shall
the enslavement of reason and
conscience continue, in countries
governed by Moslem sovereigns,
so long as the authority of the

3

Uluma receives the sanction of Moslem tradition and the universal consent of the Mohammedan fathers. " Africa's sore " will only be healed when the power of Moslem slave hunters shall be broken and when the Turk and Arab shall no longer be permitted to fill their harems with the product of the slave trade. We may not gather "grapes of thorns nor figs of thistles."

We are now prepared to enter upon a brief survey of that system of religious faith and practice which is based upon this foundation. According to Moslem authorities the faith of Islam includes seven points, enumerated in the following creed :

" I believe in God, in the Angels, in the Books, in the Apostles, in the Last Day, in the Decrees of Almighty God both as respects good and evil, and in the Resurrection after death."

Faith in God includes not only belief in his existence as a person-

al God, but especially in his absolute Unity. It excludes not only
plurality of deities, but plurality
of persons in the One God. It re-
pudiates every idea of incarnation.
It is therefore totally opposed to
the Christian doctrine of Trinity
in Unity and of the Incarnation of
God in Christ.

The seven attributes of God are
" Life, Wisdom, Power, Will, Hearing, Seeing, and Speaking." To
the Moslem, God is not first of all
a God of Wisdom, or Love, but a
God of Infinite Power. " He is,"
to quote another,* " the Lord of the
worlds, the Author of the heavens
and the earth, who hath created
life and death, in whose hands is
dominion, who maketh the dawn
to appear and causeth the night to
cover the day, the Great all-Power-
ful Lord of the Glorious Throne ;
the thunder proclaimeth his per-
fection, the whole earth is his
handful, and the heavens shall be

* Mr. Stanley Lane Pool, in Selections from
Quran.

folded together in his right hand. And with the power he conceives the knowledge that directs it to right ends. God is the wise, the just, the true, the swift in reckoning, who knoweth every ant's weight of good and of ill that each man hath done, and who suffereth not the reward of the faithful to perish."

So overwhelming indeed is the sense of the power of the Almighty that there seems to be no room left for the will of the creature, and so it comes to pass that in the minds of the majority of Moslems " God plays with humanity as on a chessboard, and works out his game without regard to the sacrifice of the pieces."

Still, on the other hand, there is a recognition of the mercy of God, though indeed it must be conceded that this is not the chief thought of Islam. The Moslem is guided by fear, rather than drawn by love. The God of Islam is undoubtedly the true God, and yet there are serious objections to the Moslem's conception of him. Not only do we object to his rejection of the Trinity, but also to his having exalted God's Omnipotence over all other attributes, to the lowering of his character for holiness—nothing being said of God's holiness in the Quran which might not be said of a holy man ; to his limiting the goodness of God to Moslems, no matter what their character, relegating even the infants of unbelievers to hell fire ; to his sacrifice of God's justice by denying the necessity for any atonement for sin ; and, finally, to his limitation of the truth of God by the sanctification of a lie, if it only be spoken in self-defense or for the advancement of Islam. It must not be forgotten that the God of Islam is not merely the Allah described in the Quran, but the God who speaks in every word, syllable, and letter of the Quran. We must not therefore separate what we conceive to have special reference to God in its teaching from what we may conceive to have been used by Mohammed for the furtherance of his private or political purposes; for, according to Islam, Mohammed was but the mouthpiece of Divinity. If, then, we would get a correct idea of the Allah of Islam we must take into account all that was done by Mohammed under the sanction of the Quran. Let this be done, and it will appear that what we have just said is by no means extravagant, or unduly severe.

On the subject of the Books recognized by Moslems, we note as of special interest their faith in 104 volumes of inspiration, revealed from time to time through the medium of the prophets, closing with the Quran. Of these it is said 100 are no longer in existence: these are the books of Adam, Seth, Enoch and Abraham. The four still extant are the Pentateuch of Moses, the Psalms of David, the Gospel of Jesus, and the Quran of Mohammed. These are all recognized by the Quran as the word of God given for a light to guide men in the way of salvation. Nevertheless, as already stated, modern Moslems regard all these, excepting the Quran, as having been corrupted. When therefore a Moslem says he believes in the books contained in the Jewish and Christian Scriptures, he means only to declare that such books were once delivered to the prophets, though now so corrupted as no longer to be worthy of credence excepting in so far as they are confirmed by the Quran.

In regard to the prophets, Moslems believe in 144,000. There are however no more than 28 whose names are given in the Quran. They also declare their belief in 315 apostles or prophets sent with some special message. Nine were exalted to the position of leaders in the ushering in of new dispensations; six of these were styled the Nabi-ul-Azim. These are Adam, Noah, Abraham, Moses,

Jesus and Mohammed. Each of these is distinguished by a special title ; thus, Adam is the Chosen of God, Noah the Prophet of God, Abraham the Friend of God, Moses the Speaker with God, Jesus the Spirit of God, and Mohammed the Apostle of God. A striking fact in this connection is that, while according to popular belief all prophets were sinless, yet, in accordance with the teaching of the Quran and the Traditions, Jesus is the only sinless prophet of Islam. Of other prophets it is said in the Quran either that they confessed and repented of their sins or that God laid certain sins to their charge. The same thing is true of the teaching of the Traditions—. especially true in the case of Mohammed, who is commanded to repent of his sins and who is said to have professed his penitence seventy times in a single day. But of Jesus, nowhere is there a line or a hint of any kind that He was ever chargeable with sin. HE IS

THE ONLY SINLESS PROPHET OF
ISLAM.

There is however no doctrine
that impresses itself more power-
fully upon the mind of Moslems
than that of the Resurrection and
the Judgment Day. To them this
is the great day of assizes. The day
will however be at least 1,000 years
in duration. Its approach will be
marked by many signs : the faith
will decay among men, wickedness
and corruption will be rampant, the
meanest persons shall be advanced
to eminent dignity, there shall be
tumults and seditions, wars and
distress in the world ; the sun shall
rise in the west, a " beast " shall
arise out of the earth, and appear
in the holy temple of Makkah,
having the head of a bull, the eye
of a hog, the ears of an elephant, the
horns of a stag, the neck of an
ostrich, the breast of a lion, the
color of a tiger, the back of a cat, the
tail of a ram, the legs of a camel,
and the voice of an ass. About this
time the Antichrist shall appear.

41

One-eyed, with the word *Kafir* or
"Infidel" written on his forehead,
he will appear in Syria riding on
a white ass, followed by 70,000
Jews, and shall continue on the
earth for fourteen months, conquer-
ing and devastating until he be destroyed by Jesus, who shall de-
scend from heaven and establish
the religion of Islam throughout
the whole world. Then the Mahdi
shall appear.

These with many other marvellous signs shall portend the near
approach of the Awful Day when
the first blast of the angel trump
shall strike terror to every heart in
heaven and earth. A second blast
will visit with death every creature
in the universe. The third trum-
pet blast of the angel, now himself
raised from the dead, will restore
all to life, when the judgment will
begin. Then shall every beast that
has suffered at the hands of a cruel
master tread upon the prostrate
form of his persecutor. Then shall
the wicked be brought forth with

blackened faces, backbiters in the form of apes, tyrants in the form of swine, hypocrites gnawing their tongues, the proud and vainglorious clad in garments daubed with pitch. These shall all be obliged to pass over a bridge so narrow that they shall slip off it into the gaping vortex of hell underneath. The righteous, by which we are to understand the faithful of every age and dispensation, shall be brought forth in honor, clad in bright and beautiful garments, seated on white - winged camels with saddles of gold. To them shall be opened the gates of Paradise, into which they will be ushered, where, seated on sofas garnished with silk and precious stones, they shall sport themselves in the companionship of the black-eyed girls of Paradise, eating the luscious fruits of Eden, drinking the spicy waters of *Al Kauthar* out of vessels of gold.

It was this vision which enabled the fiery Saracen to rush to certain death in the exultant hope of martyrdom. It is this hope which ever recruits the ranks of the Ghazies of Afghanistan or the fanatical Darwesh of the Soudan. To them warfare against infidels is a merit, while death in such a cause is a sure passport to Paradise.

We now must notice briefly the practice of the Moslem religion. It is summed up under five heads: the reading of the Kalima, observance of stated prayers, fasting, giving of legal alms, and pilgrimage to Makkah.

By reading the Kalima is meant repeating the formula *La ilah illillah wa Mohammed ur rusul ullah; i. e.,* "There is no god but Allah, and Mohammed is the apostle of Allah." This formula must be repeated at least once before death, with a sincere heart and a loud voice, in the presence of witnesses.

The duty of prayer requires the punctilious observance of five daily stated prayers. Early in the morning, at the very first streak of dawn, the Muazzin's call will announce the time for the first prayer. The next prayer must be offered at midday, the third at about three o'clock in the afternoon, the fourth at sunset, and the fifth when night has closed in. These prayers should be said in the Arabic language, and if possible the men should assemble in the Mosque for that purpose. They may be, however, and generally are, offered wherever the Moslem may be at the prayer hour. It is an impressive scene to witness Moslems as they drop their implements of daily labor and either in companies or alone spread a sheet upon the ground and proceed to say their prayers. It may be on the roadside or at a railroad station, no matter where, no matter by whom surrounded, the Moslem says his prayers. His witness for his faith is clear and unequivocal. He glories in his faith. On Friday Moslems assemble punctiliously at the Mosque, where special prayers suited to this holy day are offered.

Sometimes the service is accompanied by a discourse or sermon. Prayers over, the faithful return to their usual occupations.

The duty of fasting relates particularly to the fast of Ramadhan. This is a sacred month. During the entire month the Moslem is obliged to fast from sunrise until sunset. No morsel of food or drop of water may pass his lips during the day. This in hot climates in the long days of summer is a serious trial. Many lose their health and some their lives through the rigor of this fast. The sick and the weakly are exempted on condition they fast an equal number of days at another time. During the night the Moslem is free to eat and drink as much as he pleases. The worldly minded, if sick, escape the rigor of this fast by turning as much of the day into the night as possible.

Almsgiving (Zakat) is a kind of legal tax, corresponding in some measure to the tithe of Judaism. It is assessed variously according to the employment of the giver. It amounts to two and one half per cent. of his gains or income, and is spent in the cause of religion and the support of the poor. It must not be inferred that this is the sum total of Moslem charity. To their credit it must be said they are generous and kind to the poor and hospitable to travelers and strangers. During the late war between the Turks and the Russians the Mohammedans of India contributed large sums for the relief of the sick and wounded among their co-religionists. In one city the women even took off their ornaments of gold and silver and put them into the contribution plate.

The pilgrimage to Makkah, like the duty of prayer and fasting and almsgiving, is enjoined by the teaching of the Quran and sanctioned by the example of the prophet. Every Moslem with health and wealth sufficient to enable him to perform the pilgrimage to Makkah must do so at least once in his lifetime. The rites connected with the Hajj or Pilgrimage are a relic of Arab heathenism, but are purged of all idolatrous sentiments. The rite which most nearly approaches to the idolatrous is that of kissing the Black Stone in the corner of the Kaabah, or sacred temple at Makkah. It is recorded in one of the traditions that the Caliph Omar, when first he performed the pilgrimage after his conversion to Islam, addressed this stone thus: "Verily I know that thou art a stone ; thou dost no good or harm in the world, and if it was not that I saw the prophet kiss thee I would not kiss thee."

In addition to these practical duties of Islam we may add that of Jahad, or Crusade. This duty was recognized in the days of Mohammed. Indeed it was to the performance of it that the mission of the prophet owes its success. According to the teaching of Islam, every Moslem must hold himself ready to fight in the Way of

God. This either means to fight in defence of the faith, or, under competent guidance, to make war upon the infidels with a view to their conversion or extirpation. It is under shelter of this doctrine that Mohammedans have always felt themselves at liberty to assault any nation or tribe of unbelievers. It is under shelter of this principle that Arab slave-hunters practise their bloody work in Central Africa and Turks ruthlessly slaughter Christians in Armenia.

The recent atrocities perpetrated by Turks and Kurds in Armenia present to us a striking illustration of the terrible cruelty and fiendish outrage and slaughter which always ensue upon a *jahad* or crusade in the name of religion. That the massacres in Armenia were prompted by religious zeal and emanated from the Sultan at Constantinople and his advisers seems certain. The following extract from the statement of a Mohammedan official who made a careful inquiry as to the causes and extent of the massacres at Harpoot, Arabkir, and other places, fully confirms this view :

" A petition in behalf of Armenians was given to the powers in the hope of improving their condition. An imperial firman was issued for carrying out the reforms suggested by the powers. On this account the Turkish population was much excited by the thought that an Armenian principality was to be established, and they began to show great hostilities to the poor Armenians, who had been obedient to them and with whom they had lived in peace for more than six hundred years. In addition to their anger was added the permission and help of the government, by which, before the reforms were undertaken, the whole Turkish population was aroused to the evil intent of obliterating the Armenian name ; and then behold the Turks of the district, joining with neighboring Kurdish tribes by the thousand, armed with weapons which are allowed only to the army, and with the help and under the guidance of Turkish officials, in an open manner and in the daytime, attacking the Armenian houses, shops, stores, monasteries, churches and schools, and committing fearful atrocities.

"After plundering these places they burned many houses, churches, monasteries, schools and markets with the petroleum they had brought with them, and the large stone churches which they could not burn they ruined in other ways. Some churches were converted into mosques and devoted to Moslem worship, and books sacred to Christians were torn in pieces. Besides this, priests, laymen, women and even small children were made Moslems by force. They put white turbans on the men and cut the hair of the women in bangs like that of the Moslem women, and made them go through Moslem prayers. Married women and girls were defiled, against the sacred law, and some were married by force and are still detained in Turkish houses. Especially in Talu, Severek, Malatia, Arabkir and Choonkoosh many women and girls were taken to the soldiers' barracks and dishonored. Many, to escape such dishonor, threw themselves into the Euphrates, and some committed suicide in other ways."

The influence of centuries of culture in this kind of " holy war " is seen in the cold-blooded indifference of Moslem people everywhere. The writer says, " The strange thing about it all is that very few Moslems seemed to revolt at such deeds. Men of intelligence and education view these deeds with complacency." Many months have passed since the Christian world was horrified by the first of these massacres. Every Christian nation has voiced its protest against them. We have yet to hear a single word of disapproval from any Moslem people on earth.

This has ever been the favorite missionary agency of Islam. When certain apologists for Islam institute a comparison between the relative success of Moslem and Christian missions they ought in all fairness to compare and then carefully catalogue the means used by these missionaries and the moral results of their work.

Such, then, is the religion of Islam, at least in its fundamental principles. Like every other religion it has been influenced by the national life and customs of its votaries. Like Christianity it has been divided by schisms and heresies. There have been no less than 150 sects of Moslems. Some of these divisions have been political in their character, others doctrinal or philosophical. The great schism of the Sunni and Shiah sects dates from the earliest years of Islam and was due to a dispute as to who should be the Caliph or successor of Mohammed. The Shiahs claimed that Ali, the husband of Fatima, Mohammed's daughter, should have been the first Caliph. They therefore reject Abu Baqr, Omar and Othman, the first three caliphs, as usurpers. This political division has led to many bloody wars. The division between Persia and Turkey is yet as a wide and impassable stream.

A modern sect of considerable influence in Arabia and India is that of the Wahabbis, who have endeavored to reform many abuses and to bring back Islam to its original purity. The political power of this sect was broken by the late Mohammed Ali of Egypt.

On theological grounds Islam has had many sects. The Ali-Illahis believe that God was incarnate in the various Imaums or Leaders in all dispensations down to the time of Ali, who was the last. It is interesting to notice how the thought of incarnation of the godhead forced itself in upon the bold unitarianism of Islam. Another sect, the Mushabiites, taught that God possessed a human form. Still another held that though the body of God was human in outline yet it was a luminary body.

The discussion as to the attributes of divinity, which led to the aforementioned heresies, resulted in the rise of the Mutazalites, who may be called the liberal or rationalistic sect of Islam. This sect has been revived in India under the leadership of Sayed Amir Ali of Calcutta.

The sect of the Sufis or mystics adopt a pantheistic philosophy and endeavor to explain the Quran in accord with it. The result is an orthodox highly spiritual worship, on the one hand, and a blind fatalism, amounting to atheism, on the other. The influence of these various heterodox schools of thought upon the Moslem mind is of no small moment to the cause of Christian evangelization. These elements of Moslem nationality afford the most hopeful subjects of missionary endeavor. When, therefore, it becomes subject to a Christian power, as in India and Egypt, it loses, so to speak, its right arm.* On its theological side Islam is supported by an extensive literature and a regular system of theological instruction. In addition to this, thousands of men of no mean intellectual calibre spend their whole lives in its study and propagation. Vast institutions of learning have been established, and are still supported by the generosity of princes and kings, which educate Moslem youths without allowing them to come under any other

* The notion of patriotism is entirely subordinate to that of religion. The lawful rulers of earthly kingdoms are Moslems, who acknowledge the hierarchy at Constantinople. The Sultan is king of kings, who may kill fourteen of his subjects every day, if he will, and that without question. The Moslem owes allegiance to no other than a Moslem government. He cannot therefore be at once a faithful subject of Christian dominion and a consistent follower of *orthodox* Islam. He is always *bound* to obey the call of the Caliph to holy war. These facts cannot be too well considered by all our statesmen in their study of the Moslem problem.

religious influences. Such a religion, holding sway over one-eighth
of the population of the globe, second only to Christianity in numer-
ical strength among the religions
of the world, occupying the chief
centres of influence in the Eastern
world, commands our respect, in
spite of its appalling errors, while
it forces upon us the conviction
that it is, as we have already said,
the principal rival of our holy religion.

Does it not then seem a little
strange that, what with our missions to Mormons and Jews, our
churches in America have hardly
thought of a special mission to
Moslems? True it is that men are
sent to India, Egypt, and Turkey
and Persia, who in the providence
of God are led to devote themselves specially to the Moslems; and
yet the churches and even boards
of missions seem to think of Moslems very much as they do of the
heathen elsewhere. But this is
not enough. It is only reasonable

to require of missionaries sent to Moslem lands such preparation for their work as shall enable them to at least understand the thoughts and feelings of these followers of the false prophet, and so be able to direct them intelligently to the truth of that gospel which is attested by the Quran, and to the claims of that Saviour who is the Sinless Prophet of Islam, and whom they confess to be now exalted in heaven, and who is to come again to establish the true religion of God upon the earth.

We do not wish to be understood as disparaging what has been done for the work of missions among Moslems. We only desire to advocate an improvement of method. We would plead for a more thorough and systematic training of men for work among Mohammedans everywhere.

The question is sometimes asked, What is the influence of Mohammedanism upon the moral character of Moslems? In reply to this question, it must be admitted that wherever it brings to its allegiance a grossly idolatrous people, especially if they be fetish or devil worshippers, it does raise their moral status. Cannibalism and infanticide are abolished; idolatrous customs, degrading and immoral, are obliterated; certain fixed rules are enforced in respect to society and the State; thieves and murderers are severely punished; the use of intoxicating drinks is greatly diminished if not absolutely prevented; children are educated to some extent and trained up as the worshippers of the true God; certain ideas of honor, courage and devotion are inculcated, and so the scale of morality is greatly advanced; and yet there is a limit to Moslem progress in morals a long way this side the goal of Christian ethics. The permissions of the Quran in respect to polygamy, concubinage and divorce, the sanction of slavery and holy war, the example of Mohammed himself, the adoption of the principle that the end justifies the means—thereby consecrating every form of deception and lying, every sort of persecution and violence to the cause of religion—these things effectually block the wheels of progress in ethical spheres, so that Moslem nations have hardly ever reached even the planes of moral purity occupied by the most degenerate Christian nations. The difference between the immoral Christian and the immoral Moslem may be thus described: the Christian is immoral in spite of his religion; the Moslem is immoral because of his religion. It is, indeed, chiefly owing to this cause that Moslem empires are not enduring. The social and national life is undermined by a fatal disease, which, like leprosy, festers and rots, though the life may be long continued.

Another question has been asked; namely, whether Islam has accomplished good to the world. Aside from the *a priori* argument that the

Lord, who has all power in heaven
and earth, overrules all things for
good to his church, we think the
history of the world will show that,
while Islam has wrought the ma-
terial ruin of every people she has
conquered, yet she has been made
the instrument of accomplishing a
good deal towards the spiritual
and intellectual advancement of
the world. She has ever been a
scourge to idolaters in the church
and out of it. She has borne witness to a living, personal God in
the midst of generations of hea-
thens, moulding their language
and thought in monotheistic forms,
breaking up powerful systems of
heathenism, and thus in a sense
preparing the way of the Lord.
Thus has she been used by God to
accomplish his purposes. Every
reader of church history knows
how much the success of the Reformation was due to the presence
of the Turk at Constantinople.
Islam has been a hammer in the
hand of the Almighty wherewith

he has smitten his enemies. That work seems to have been accomplished. The nations ruled by the Moslems have lost their prestige and seem to be doomed to speedy subjection to Christian powers. Their power to destroy and to persecute has already been considerably curtailed. Almost one-half of the Moslems of the world are now under Christian rule. Among them the gospel is preached by the peaceful messengers of Christ without fear. Those who choose to abjure Islam are free to profess their faith in Christ without fear of bastinado or death. Not only so, but Islam is being honeycombed by influences which have greatly weakened its hold upon its own adherents. What with Babism in Persia, Wahabbiism in Arabia, Syed-Ahmadism in India, Mahdiism in Egypt and Central Africa, Islam is sorely rent by internal dissensions. Not least important is the influence of Protestant Christianity through its missions and educational institutions. In Syria, Turkey, Egypt. and Persia many thoughtful Moslems are studying the Word of God. Some believe, though unable to make a public profession of their faith. In India many hundreds of the followers of Islam have publicly abjured that faith and been received into the church. Thousands of Moslem youths are being educated in Christian schools. Many of the teachers in these schools and many of the most eloquent and learned of the native ministers in the church were once the votaries of Islam. The leaven is already working in this mass, and our hope is that it may speedily leaven the whole lump.

The Moslems have a tradition that when Masih-ud-Dajjal, the Antichrist, shall sorely press the Moslems " all on a sudden prayers will begin, and Jesus, Son of Mary, will come down and act as Imaum, or Leader, to them. And when Dajjal, this enemy of God, shall see Jesus, he will fear to be near, dissolving away like salt in water. And if Jesus lets him alone, verily he will melt and perish, and God will kill him by the hand of Jesus." Let us hope the day is not far distant when Jesus shall indeed become the Leader of these multitudes, and that the forces of Antichrist shall melt away like salt in water and perish before " the sword of his Spirit " and " the brightness of his coming."

www.ingramcontent.com/pod-product-compliance
Lightning Source LLC
Chambersburg PA
CBHW021523090426
42739CB00007B/750